Contents

Living with electricity

This is a kitchen from 100 years ago.
Nothing uses electricity.

⭐ Draw a modern kitchen.
Put in lots of appliances that use electricity.

⭐ Make a list of all the appliances.

⭐ Now complete Task Sheet 1.

Task 2 Being safe

Electricity can hurt or even kill you.
You have to be very careful.

- **Never touch live wires.**
- **Never touch plugs and switches with wet hands.**

✴ Look at the pictures.

✴ List all the dangerous things you can see.

✴ Complete Task Sheet 2.

3

Battery power

The electricity from small batteries is weak.
Small batteries are safe to use.

✴ What things use small batteries?

✴ Make a list.

✴ Look inside some safe battery-powered devices.
How many batteries do they need?
Which way do the batteries face?

✴ Now complete Task Sheet 3.

Battery care

Although batteries are safe to use, you must still be careful.

Here are some rules:

- **Never open batteries.**
- **Never connect them incorrectly – they can get hot.**
- **Never put a battery in your mouth.**
- **Always get rid of used batteries properly.**

✹ List all the things that Sparky is doing wrong.

✹ Explain why they are wrong.

Make the bulb light

- ✴ Make a circuit to light up a bulb.

- ✴ How many wires will you need?

- ✴ Remember, it must be complete to work.

- ✴ Draw the circuit you have made.

YOU NEED:

battery and battery holder

bulb holder   *bulb*

wires

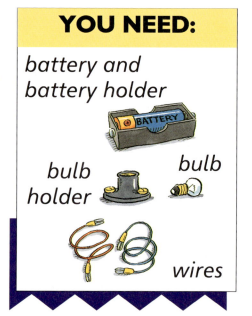

- ✴ Now try Task Sheet 4.

Make the buzzer buzz

"Buzzers are special,"
says Sparky.
"You must connect them
the right way round."

Is he right?

* Take the bulb out of
your circuit.
Put a buzzer in.
Try it both ways round.

* Draw the circuit.

* Explain what happens.

YOU NEED:

*battery and
battery holder*

buzzer

wires

What's inside a light bulb?

A light bulb has a thin wire inside it.
When electricity flows through it,
the wire glows. Remember,
only a complete circuit
lets the electricity flow.

* Look at the
light bulb.
Can you see
the thin wire?

* Complete Task Sheet 5.

A bulb holder

There are two ways to light a torch:

- hold the wires against the base of the torch bulb
  or
- join the wires to a bulb holder.

✸ Look at the picture.

✸ Follow the path of the electricity through the bulb.

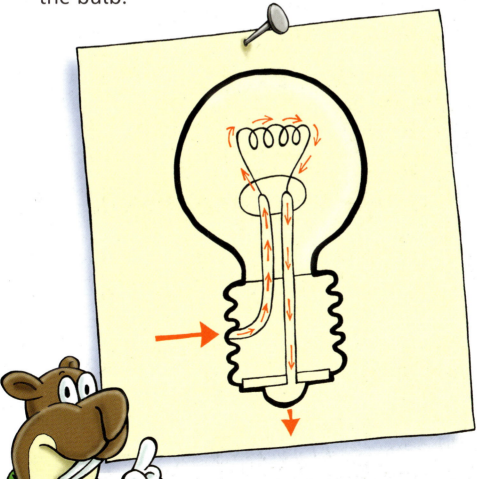

Task 9 Why won't they work?

Sparky has been drawing circuits.

⭐ Which ones will work?

⭐ Which ones won't work?

⭐ How can Gordon make all the circuits work?

⭐ Now complete Task Sheet 6.

Inside a torch

There are connections at each end of a battery.

⭐ Look inside a torch.

⭐ Find the batteries.

⭐ Can you see the connections?

⭐ Which way round are they?

⭐ What would happen if one was the wrong way round?

⭐ Match each word to the correct box.

A glass ball with a
fine wire inside that
glows when electricity
goes through it.

This buzzes when
electricity goes
through it.

bulb-
holder

battery

buzzer

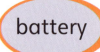

bulb

A source of
electrical energy.

This holds a bulb so
that wires can be
easily connected.

More electricity words

⭐ Match each word to the correct box.

⭐ Make a table of all the electrical words you know and their meaning.

complete circuit

A long thin piece of metal that carries electricity from place to place. Often covered in plastic.

switch

This controls the electricity – letting it through or stopping it.

wire

This allows electricity to go all the way round and do something on the way.

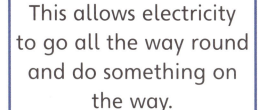

Make these circuits

Sparky has finished three circuits.

✳ Make his circuits.

✳ Follow his instructions carefully.

YOU NEED:

battery and battery holder

bulb holder

wires

buzzer

Find it!

⭐ Look at this page.

⭐ Find:

- a machine that uses electricity
- something dangerous
- a circuit where the bulb will not work
- a complete buzzer circuit.

⭐ Now complete Task Sheet 7.

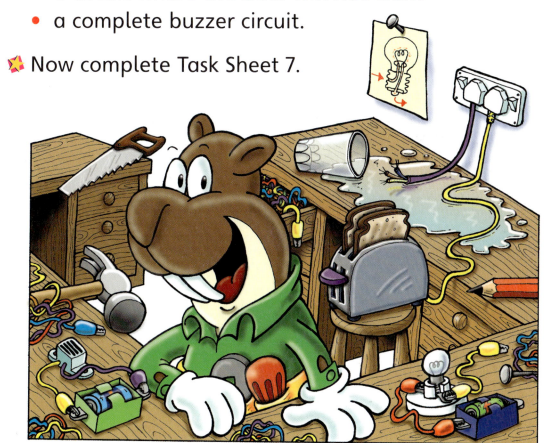

Guess What?

It's quick and it's powerful
It doesn't make a sound.
It comes into your house
Through wires underground.
You can't hear or see it
So what could it be?
I'll give you a clue:
It begins with an E.

What useful things can you think
of that use batteries or mains electricity?